Collins

1000 English Words

Our Home Activity Book

Rebecca Adlard

illustrated by Duc Nguyen

Contents

How to use this book 3
Where we live 4–5
In the bedroom 6–7
In the bathroom. 8–9
In the living room. 10–11
In the kitchen 12–13
In the home office 14–15
The garden at night 16–17
Mix it up! 18–19
Sort it! 20–21
More fun! 22–23
Let's play! 24–25
Let's create and read! 26
Let's write! 27
Answers 28–31
Word list 32

How to use this book

Hello!

In this book, there are lots of games and fun activities to help you practise English words.

Before you start, you can think about what words you know for each topic. You can make a word map and add new words from this book.

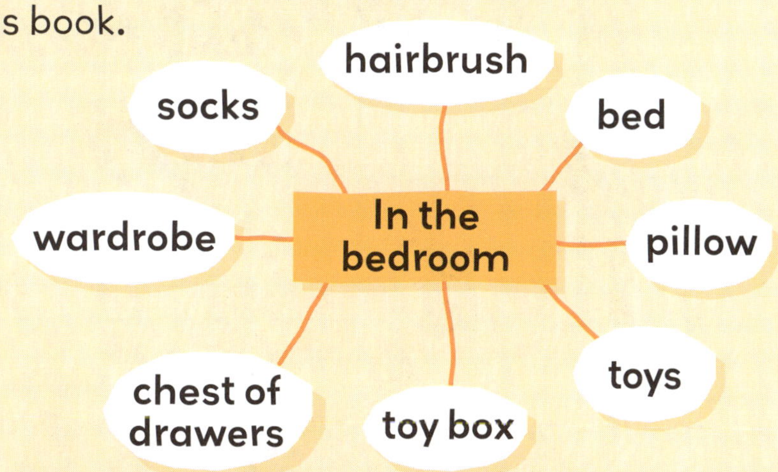

Oscar and Mia are here to help you. How many times can you find them in this book?

- When you see this ⭐, there's an extra activity from Oscar and Mia.
- When you see this ❓, you can learn an interesting fact. Tell your friends and family!
- When you see this, go to **collins.co.uk/eltresources** for extra fun.
- Use the word list on page 32 and tick ✓ all the words you learn!

And when you finish a game or activity, you can check your answers on pages 28–31.

All the words from this book can be found fully illustrated in *Collins 1000 English Words* visual dictionary.

You can go to **collins1000englishwords.com** to find a glossary with audio.

Where we live

Spot the difference

Circle eight differences in Picture B. Can you find Mia and Oscar in the pictures?

A

B

Bonus point

Can you say the things that are different in the pictures?

My street. Go online to spot the things in your street!

Picture puzzle

Write the words in this picture puzzle. Use the word in the blue squares to complete the sentence below the puzzle.

I live at number ______________ .

Follow the lines

Who is going to the house? Follow the lines and write the answer.

In the bedroom

Photo scramble

What can you see in the bedroom? Use the letters to make words.

1 
staincur

2 
wilpol

3 
dbe

4 
vedtu

5 
droberaw

6 
stech fo rewsdra

7 
yot xob

8 
gru

9 
pressilp

Crack the code

Write the letter for each picture to find what clothes are in the wardrobe.

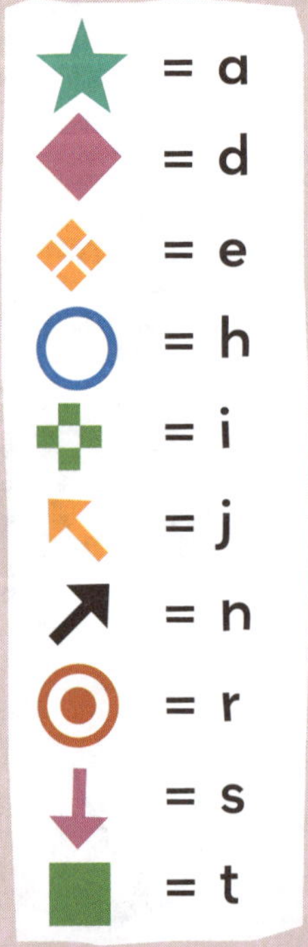

Toy word circles

Use each letter in the circle to make a toy word.
Start with the letter in the middle of the circle.

d y **t** e d

l l **d** o

Let's draw!
Go online to draw a picture of your bedroom.

t b **r** o o

Did you know?
The First World Hotel in Malaysia is the largest hotel in the world. It has more than 7,350 bedrooms!

How many toys?

How many dolls ☐, teddies ☐ and robots ☐ are there?
Name the other things you see.

In the bathroom

Which words?

Tick the words that you can spell using the letters in **bathroom.**

- bath ☐
- tap ☐
- room ☐
- bathmat ☐
- brush ☐
- wash ☐
- dry ☐
- arm ☐

Wordmatch

Match the word parts to make four more bathroom words.

tooth	cloth
bath	board
cup	mat
toi	brush
face	let

Wordsearch

Can you find the bathroom words in the wordsearch?

b	e	r	s	t	p	w	o	b	t	o	o
m	r	t	o	w	e	l	q	a	o	e	b
i	o	r	a	i	l	u	f	t	o	j	r
r	w	s	p	w	k	o	t	h	t	p	s
r	t	p	y	g	s	j	k	m	h	f	m
s	h	o	w	e	r	v	z	a	p	p	i
s	t	n	q	v	p	y	x	t	a	j	r
c	x	j	i	h	g	u	q	d	s	x	r
o	t	f	a	c	e	c	l	o	t	h	o
m	s	h	a	m	p	o	o	k	e	m	r
b	t	p	f	a	c	x	c	l	a	e	p
x	t	o	o	t	h	b	r	u	s	h	m

mirror

comb

shower

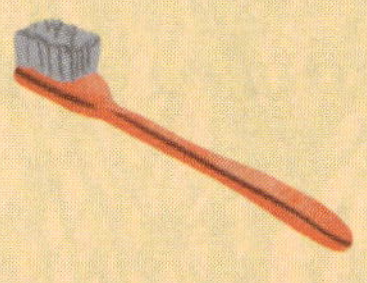

toothbrush

toothpaste

face cloth

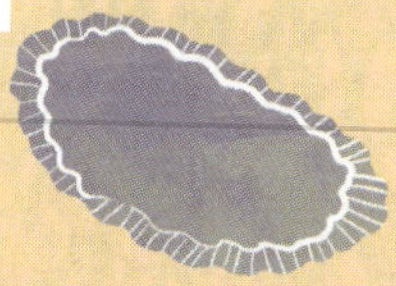

bathmat

shampoo

soap

towel

In the living room

Wordsnake

Find and circle five things Oscar and Mia have got in their living room.

Odd one out

Find and cross out (x) the odd one out. Draw lines to match to the topic.

sofa	armchair	bookcase	cushion
ball	book	comic	magazine
watch television	cook dinner	read a comic	play a board game

- Things you do in the living room
- Things you sit on in the living room
- Things you read in the living room

Bonus point

Can you add one more thing to each list?

Things you do: ______

Things you sit on: ______

Things you read: ______

Wordsearch

Can you find and write the living room words in the wordsearch?

p	c	u	s	h	i	o	n	m	f	b	h	m	p	e
l	f	a	f	m	u	y	v	d	e	o	v	n	i	v
m	b	n	t	r	n	t	c	e	l	o	u	e	c	h
o	g	u	y	j	v	t	z	q	j	k	d	c	t	p
t	e	l	e	v	i	s	i	o	n	d	g	a	u	e
u	n	n	d	x	c	q	b	p	z	x	o	r	r	n
b	o	o	k	c	a	s	e	n	c	t	o	p	e	f
m	k	g	f	o	r	j	o	d	v	a	s	e	v	j
x	n	w	p	r	f	k	h	e	k	b	t	t	h	l
s	s	o	f	a	n	b	a	v	b	l	l	d	g	a
m	r	x	l	w	u	p	o	r	l	e	x	q	c	m
a	h	o	q	o	f	l	e	z	g	h	c	e	b	p
y	u	b	j	d	g	a	b	m	d	v	c	r	l	y
z	c	o	m	i	c	n	h	v	h	c	l	o	c	k
u	n	k	y	r	c	t	m	l	l	f	b	n	r	f

In the kitchen

Find the word

What are the words?

1. freezer
2. cooker
3. scales
4. radio
5. kettle
6. dishwasher
7. fridge
8. microwave

Did you know?

What do you think is older: the dishwasher or the fridge? The dishwasher is old: it is more than 150 years old, but the fridge is older because it is nearly 200 years old! That's old!

Picture clues

Use the picture clues to find Oscar and Mia's favourite breakfasts. Write the first letter of each word. Example:

car = c

Oscar's favourite breakfast is ______________.

Mia's favourite breakfast is ______________.

Did you know?

People are the only living things that cook food.

In the home office

Crossword

Use the picture clues to complete the crossword with home office words.

Down

1

3

4

5

6

8

Across

2

4

7

9

10

11

Vowels

Write the vowels to make words for things you might find in a home office.

a i u e o

d _ ct _ _ n _ ry

b _ tt _ ry

c _ lc _ l _ t _ r

l _ pt _ p

s _ ck _ t

_ nv _ l _ p _

Crack the code

Write the letter for each picture to find what Mia is doing in the home office.

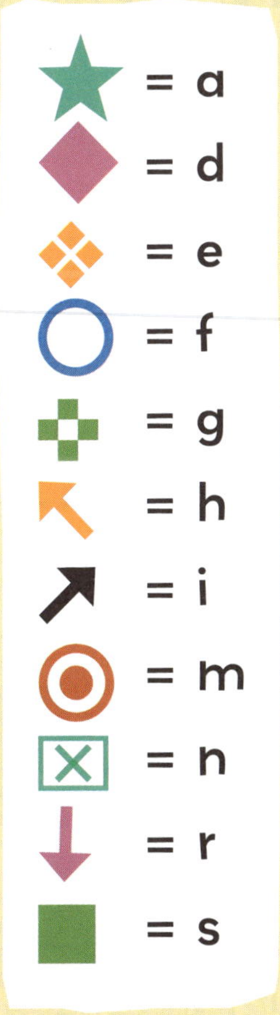

Fun with code! Go online to write in code about something in your bedroom.

The garden at night

Wordsnake

Find and write five things Oscar and Mia have got in their garden.

Bonus point

Do you have a garden? Tick (✓) the things you have got in your garden, too.

Spell it right

Which number has the correct letters to spell **TELESCOPE**?

1. STLEPSOEE
2. PSEECTLEOP
3. LEEEETLSP
4. PETLSEECO
5. CCOPELESS

Did you know?

The word 'telescope' comes from the Greek language. 'Tele' means 'a long way away' and 'scope' means 'looker'. So a telescope is a long-way-away-looker. We use telescopes to look at space, which really is a long way away.

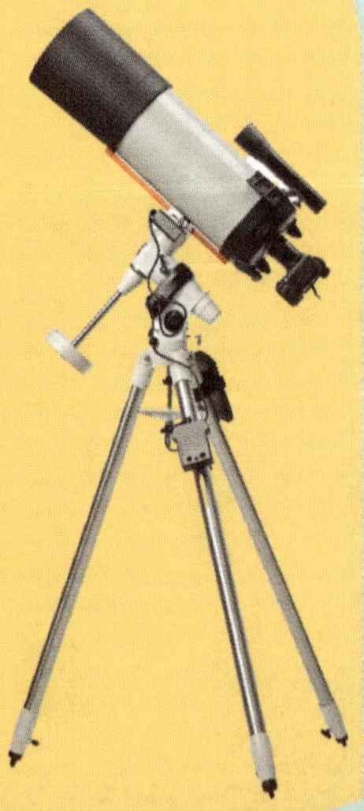

Night wordsearch

Can you find the words below in the wordsearch?

space rocket

fire

torch

b	f	i	r	e	e	s	r
e	i	g	h	t	e	p	n
m	k	x	b	j	f	a	m
o	t	o	s	t	v	c	s
o	w	d	e	o	g	e	t
n	o	c	o	r	j	r	a
s	m	v	e	c	t	o	r
f	d	t	j	h	x	c	n
k	i	l	h	t	i	k	r
s	h	a	d	o	w	e	r
f	x	s	p	j	i	t	c

moon

star

shadow

Star maps. Go online to find stars in the sky at night.

Bonus point

Which things in the wordsearch **do not** give light?

Maze

Help Oscar and Mia get through the maze to their tent.

Mix it up!

Odd one out

Find and cross out (x) the odd word out. Draw lines to match to the topic.

bed	wardrobe	chest of drawers	fridge	In the garden
armchair	duvet	sofa	cushion	In the home office
bath	pond	wall	shed	In the bathroom
laptop	dishwasher	printer	computer	In the living room
bathmat	shower	cooker	toilet	In the bedroom

Wordsquares

Cross out (✗) any letter that is in the square more than one time. What is the word?

1

N	R	T
E	I	H
R	E	G

Clue: The opposite of day.

2

B	S	D
R	L	A
L	E	S

Clue: You eat this for breakfast.

3

I	H	T
O	D	R
S	D	O

Clue: You wear this.

4

E	S	A
I	U	H
O	A	I

Clue: You live in this.

Bonus point

Make your own wordsquare with a 5-letter word from this book.

Answer: ________

Follow the lines

Follow the lines to find where each person in the family is.

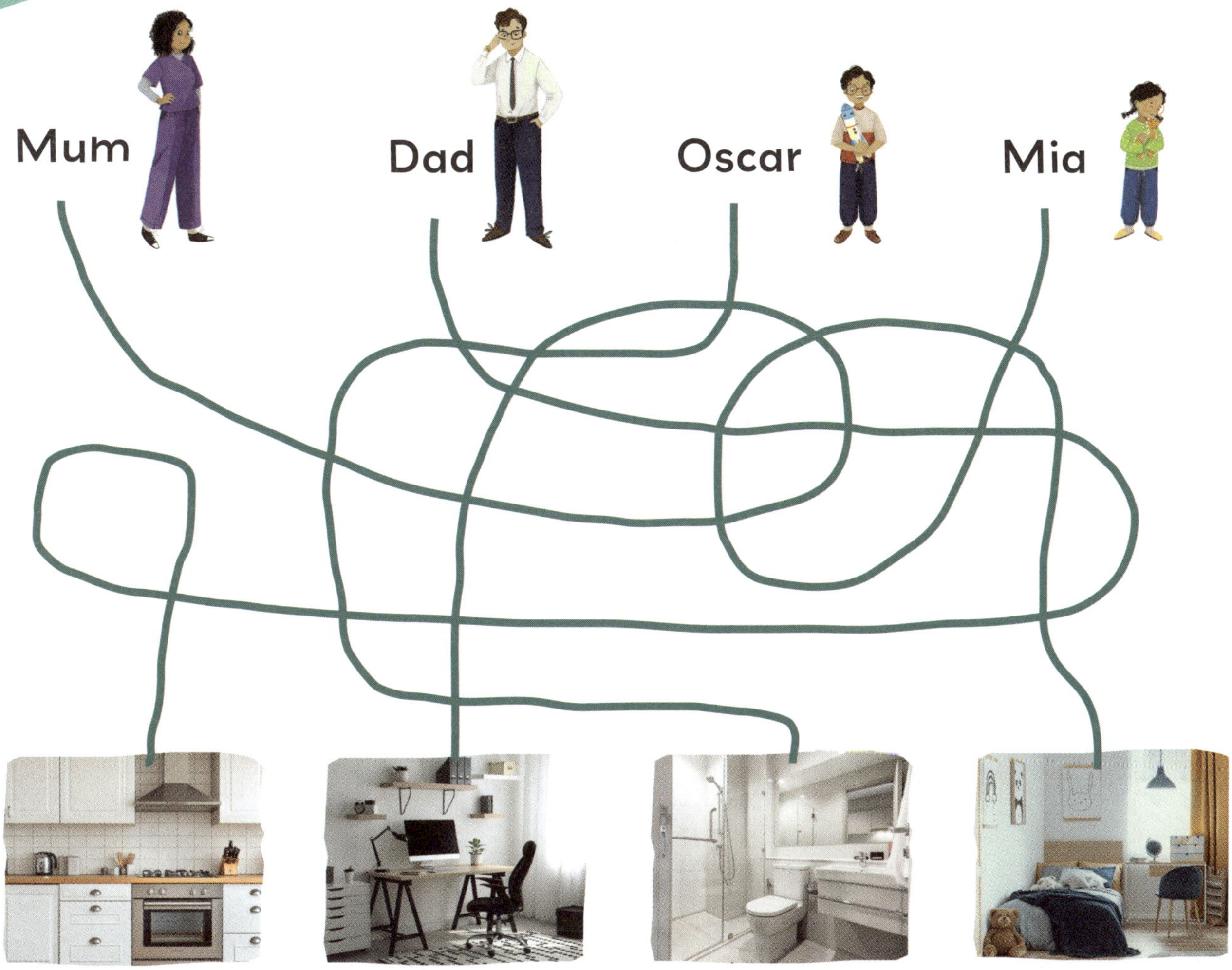

Mum is in the ______________.

Dad is in the ______________.

Oscar is in the ______________.

Mia is in the ______________.

True or false?

Answer the questions. Use the information about which room each person is in.

1. Mum is online.

   True ☐ False ☐

2. Dad is brushing his teeth.

   True ☐ False ☐

3. Oscar is in bed.

   True ☐ False ☐

4. Mia is putting on her pyjamas.

   True ☐ False ☐

Sort it!

Help Chester the robot use the letters to make words.
Then, match the words 1–16 to the pictures a–p.
Write the number in the box below the picture.

1. lowet towel
2. veno
3. moposha
4. argss
5. ecaf thocl
6. drabe
7. posa
8. anp
9. shrubootth
10. shawngi cemhina
11. raddel
12. tetlke
13. lpnta top
14. atb
15. mja
16. shub

Did you know?
Bats sleep upside down.

a

b

c

d

e

f

g

h

i

j

1

k

l

m

n

o

p

Bonus point

Now write where you can find each thing.

KITCHEN	BATHROOM	GARDEN
kettle	shampoo	plant pot

More fun!

The letter t game

Find your way around the game board. You can use a pencil or your finger. Only move on the pictures of things that start with the letter t. You can move right →, left ←, down ↓ and up ↑!

Bonus point Can you name all the things in the game that start with the letter t?

Home word circles

Use each letter in the circle to make a home word. Start with the letter in the middle of the circle.

c h k t e i h

Clue: It has an oven and a fridge.

____

o s c u i h n

Clue: You sit on it on the sofa.

____

t e o c p m u r

Clue: It's in the home office. It has a keyboard, a mouse and a screen.

____

d e a g r n

Clue: It's not in your house. It has trees.

____

e f i o f c

Clue: It's the room your mum or dad can work in at home.

____

Did you know?

Some people's homes are in caves. Would you like to live in a cave house?

Let's play!

Our home board game

Play the game with your family or friends, you need 2–4 players.
Say the words in English.

Let's play!
Go online to make your own game spinner!

You need:

How to play

- Start on the START square.
- Player 1. Spin the spinner.
- Count and move the number on the spinner.
- Name the thing in the picture. Each picture has a colour for the topic. Check the key!
- Player 2. It's your turn.
- The winner is the first player to get to the FINISH square. How many words did you know?

Key: Garden | Living room | Kitchen | Bathroom | Bedroom

Let's create and read!

Our home story

Use the clues to complete the story with your own words.

Grandma and grandad have got a new house. It is number ________ (a number). It has got a ________ (a colour) door and ________ (a number) windows. It is a ________ (big or small) house. Downstairs, there is a ________ (name of a room), a ________ (name of a room) and a ________ (name of a room). Upstairs, there is a bathroom and ________ (a number) bedrooms. Grandma likes the living room because in the living room there is a ________ (something in a living room). Grandad likes the kitchen because in the kitchen there is a ________ (something in a kitchen). They both like the garden. They like to sit in the garden at night and look at the ________ (something you see in a garden at night). They are happy in their new home.

Bonus point

Read your story out loud to your family and friends.

Let's write!

Our home kriss kross

Write all the words in the squares. Use the number of letters to help you.

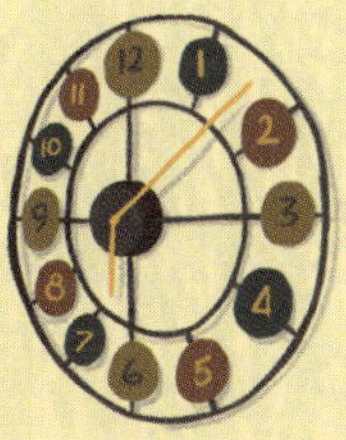

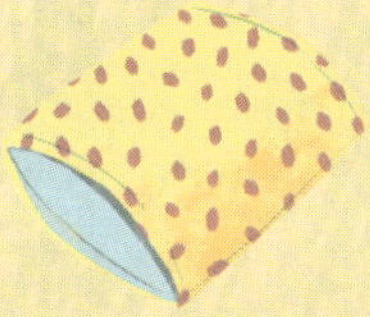

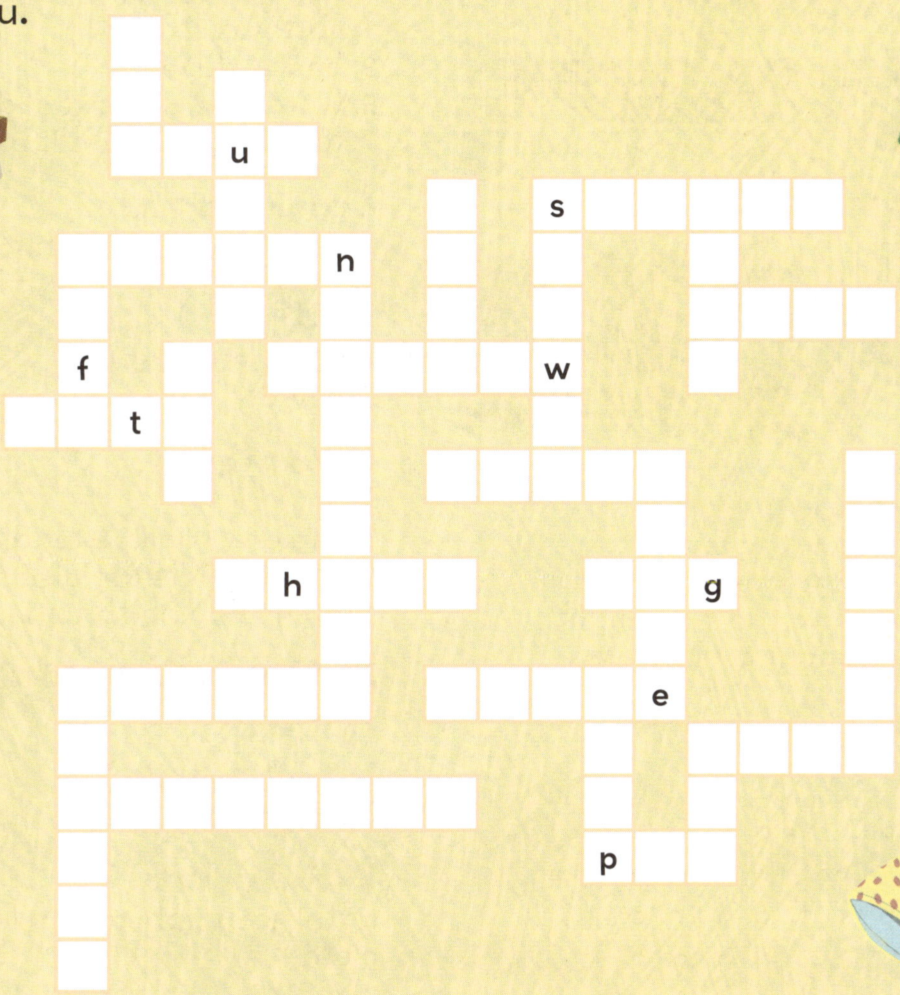

three letters
bat
bed
cup
pen
rug
van

four letters
bath
bowl
dark
gate
lamp
plug
roof
sofa
vase

five letters
duvet
house
photo
table
torch

six letters
coffee
flower
fridge
pillow
screen
shadow
shower

eight letters
internet

nine letters
neighbour

Answers

Where we live

Page 4

Spot the difference

Bonus point

the window, the fence,
the door, the postal worker,
the post box, the streetlight,
the neighbour and the van

Page 5

Picture puzzle

1 d	o	o	r	m	a	t							
						2 h	o	u	s	e			
	3 u	p	s	t	a	i	r	s					
						4 r	o	o	f				
				5 l	e	t	t	e	r	b	o	x	
						y							
				6 g	a	t	e						
				7 d	o	w	n	s	t	a	i	r	s
				8 d	o	o	r	b	e	l	l		

I live at number thirty-two.

Follow the lines

the postal worker

In the bedroom

Page 6

Photo scramble

1. curtains, 2. pillow,
3. bed, 4. duvet,
5. wardrobe, 6. chest of drawers,
7. toy box, 8. rug, 9. slippers

Crack the code

dress, jeans, t-shirt, shirt

Page7

Toy word circles

teddy, doll, robot

How many toys?

T

There are 8 dolls, 9 teddies and 2 robots. There are also socks, slippers and hairbrushes.

In the bathroom

Page 8

Which words?

bath, room, arm

Wordmatch

bathmat, cupboard, toilet, face cloth

Page 9

Wordsearch

b	e	r	s	t	p	w	o	b	t	o	o
m	r	t	o	w	e	l	q	a	o	e	b
i	o	r	a	i	l	u	f	t	o	j	r
r	w	s	p	w	k	o	t	h	t	p	s
r	t	p	y	g	s	j	k	m	h	f	m
s	h	o	w	e	r	v	z	a	p	p	i
s	t	n	q	v	p	y	x	t	a	j	r
c	x	j	i	h	g	u	q	d	s	x	r
o	t	f	a	c	e	c	l	o	t	h	o
m	s	h	a	m	p	o	o	k	e	m	r
b	t	p	f	a	c	x	c	l	a	e	p
x	t	o	o	t	h	b	r	u	s	h	m

In the living room

Page 10

Wordsnake

bookcase, board game, remote control, armchair, photo

Odd one out

bookcase – the others are things you sit on in the living room
ball – the others are things you read in the living room
cook dinner – the others are things you do in the living room

Page 11

Wordsearch

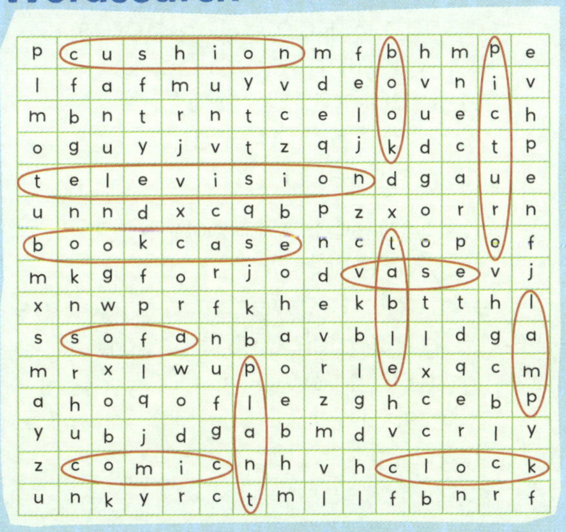

In the kitchen

Page 12

Find the word

1. freezer, 2. cooker, 3. scales, 4. radio, 5. kettle, 6. dishwasher, 7. fridge, 8. microwave

Page 13

Picture clues

Oscar's favourite breakfast is cereal.
Cereal: car, egg, roof, egg, armchair, lamp
Mia's favourite breakfast is toast.
Toast: tree, orange, avocado, sofa, tree

In the home office

Page 14

Crossword

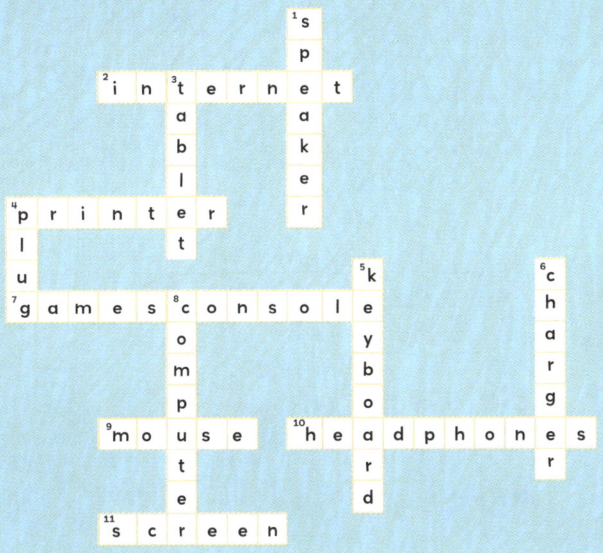

Page 15

Vowels

dictionary,
battery,
calculator,
laptop,
socket,
envelope

Crack the code

Mia is messaging friends.

The garden at night

Page 16

Wordsnake

grass, bush, pond, shed, ladder

Spell it right

4. PETLSEECO = TELESCOPE

Page 17

Night wordsearch

b	f	i	r	e	e	s	r
e	i	g	h	t	e	p	n
m	k	x	b	j	f	a	m
o	t	o	s	t	v	c	s
o	w	d	e	o	g	e	t
n	o	c	o	r	j	r	a
s	m	v	e	c	t	o	r
f	d	t	j	h	x	c	n
k	i	l	h	t	i	k	r
s	h	a	d	o	w	e	r
f	x	s	p	j	i	t	c

Bonus point

shadow, space rocket

Maze

More fun!

Page 18

Odd one out

fridge – the others are all things you find in the bedroom
duvet – the others are all things you find in the living room
bath – the others are all things you find in the garden
dishwasher – the others are all things you find in the home office
cooker – the others are all things you find in the bathroom

Wordsquares

1. night, 2. bread, 3. shirt, 4. house

Page 19

Follow the lines

Mum is in the home office.
Dad is in the kitchen.
Oscar is in the bathroom.
Mia is in the bedroom.

True or false?

1. T
2. F – Dad is in the kitchen.
3. F – Oscar is in the bathroom.
4. T

Pages 20–21

Sort it!

1. towel, 2. oven, 3. shampoo, 4. grass, 5. face cloth, 6. bread, 7. soap, 8. pan, 9. toothbrush, 10. washing machine, 11. ladder, 12. kettle, 13. plant pot, 14. bat, 15. jam, 16. bush

a. shampoo 3; b. kettle 12; c. oven 2; d. plant pot 13; e. bread; 6 f. washing machine 10; g. face cloth 5; h. soap 7; i. pan 8; j. towel 1; k. bush 16; l. bat 14; m. jam 15; n. grass 4; o. ladder 11; p. toothbrush 9

Bonus point

KITCHEN
kettle, oven, bread, washing machine, pan, jam

BATHROOM
shampoo, face cloth, soap, towel, toothbrush

GARDEN
plant pot, bush, bat, grass, ladder

Page 22

The letter t game

Bonus point

towel, teddy, toothbrush, trousers, tap, , tent, torch, telescope, toilet, table, tablet, tea, T-shirt

Page 23

Home word circles

kitchen, cushion, computer, garden, office

Let's play!

Pages 24–25

Our home board game

1. trousers,
2. sofa,
3. cup,
4. toothbrush,
5. bat,
6. dress,
7. plant,
8. milk,
9. mirror,
10. moon,
11. pillow,
12. mobile phone,
13. honey,
14. toothpaste,
15. shed,
16. hairbrush,
17. lamp,
18. egg,
19. towel,
20. star,
21. slippers,
22. picture,
23. jam,
24. tap,
25. torch,
26. teddy

Let's write!

Page 27

Our home kriss kross

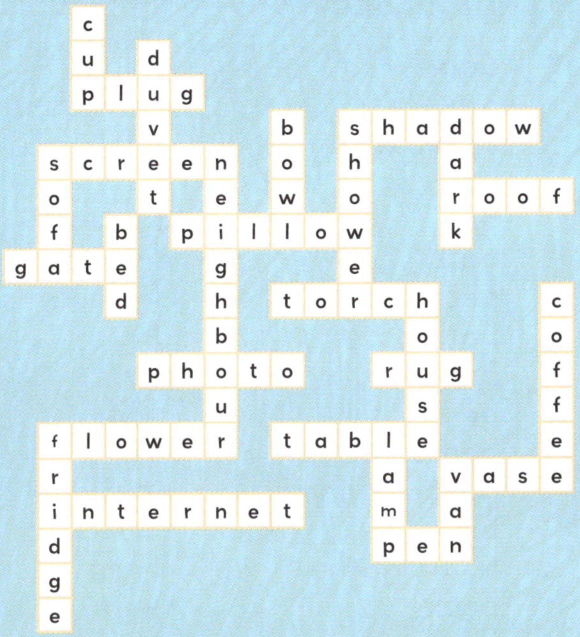

Word list

Do you know all the words in this book? Tick them when you learn them! To check the meaning and hear the words, go to **collins1000englishwords.com**

- apple
- arm
- armchair
- ball
- bat
- bath
- bathmat
- bathroom
- battery
- bed
- bedroom
- [to] be online
- big
- board game
- book
- bookcase
- bowl
- bread
- breakfast
- [to] brush
- bush
- calculator
- car
- cave
- cereal
- charger
- chest of drawers
- clock
- coffee
- comb
- comic
- computer
- [to] cook
- cooker
- cup
- cupboard
- curtain
- cushion
- dark
- delivery driver
- dictionary
- dinner
- dishwasher
- doll
- door
- doorbell
- doormat
- downstairs
- dress
- dry
- duvet
- egg
- envelope
- face cloth
- fence
- fire
- flower
- fridge
- friend
- games console
- garden
- gate
- grandad
- grandma
- grass
- hairbrush
- happy
- headphones
- honey
- hotel
- house
- internet
- jam
- jeans
- kettle
- keyboard
- kitchen
- ladder
- lamp
- laptop
- letter box
- light
- living room
- [to] look
- magazine
- microwave
- milk
- mirror
- mobile phone
- moon
- mouse
- neighbour
- night
- number
- office
- orange
- oven
- pen
- photo
- picture
- pillow
- plant
- plant pot
- [to] play
- plug
- pond
- postal worker
- postbox
- printer
- pyjamas
- radio
- [to] read
- remote control
- robot
- roof
- rug
- scales
- screen
- shadow
- shampoo
- shed
- shirt
- shower
- slipper
- soap
- sock
- socket
- sofa
- space rocket
- speaker
- star
- street
- streetlight
- table
- tablet
- tap
- tea
- teddy
- teeth
- telescope
- television
- tent
- toast
- toilet
- toothbrush
- toothpaste
- torch
- towel
- toy
- toy box
- tree
- trousers
- T-shirt
- upstairs
- van
- vase
- wall
- wardrobe
- [to] wash
- washing machine
- [to] watch
- window